The Looking House

[handwritten inscription:]
For Barbara
with love
+
delight in our
lives as they
criss + cross
[signature] 12/
/16

Other Books by Fred Marchant

POETRY

Tipping Point
Full Moon Boat
House on Water, House in Air

TRANSLATION

From a Corner of My Yard by Tran Dang Khoa
    Co-translated with Nguyen Ba Chung

EDITOR

Another World Instead: The Early Poems of William Stafford, 1937–1947

THE LOOKING HOUSE

Poems

Fred Marchant

Graywolf Press

Publication of this volume is made possible in part by a grant provided by the Minnesota State Arts Board, through an appropriation by the Minnesota State Legislature; a grant from the Wells Fargo Foundation Minnesota; and a grant from the National Endowment for the Arts, which believes that a great nation deserves great art. Significant support has also been provided by the Bush Foundation; Target; the McKnight Foundation; and other generous contributions from foundations, corporations, and individuals. To these organizations and individuals we offer our heartfelt thanks.

Published by Graywolf Press
250 Third Avenue North, Suite 600
Minneapolis, Minnesota 55401
All rights reserved.

www.graywolfpress.org

Published in the United States of America

ISBN 978-1-55597-528-9

4 6 8 9 7 5 3

Library of Congress Control Number: 2008941978

Cover design: Kyle G. Hunter

Cover photo: N. Aujoulat—CNP—MCC. Lascaux, Plafond du Diverticule axial.

For
Stefi Rubin
and
John F. Deane

Contents

III

The Looking House

House on Water, House in Air

Those places kept, where we keep
and where we can't, the river.
Where the riverbank is firm,
but crumbling, where the slate
of long ages shows bones dissolving.

Along these a boy among the living
thinks that nothing is near, or worth
believing in. That every bit of air
comes from where he will never get
and the house, lifted from its mooring,
feels like his soul in longing,

while in the room remain traces
of the adult, the underwear scattered,
a few brown drops of blood, a corpse
set loose, rolling on the floor,
in this house made of air,
house nailed by less than dream,

house that drifts with the flood of all
he thought he wanted, house that floats
on a muddy river in spring-time flood,
house like a human head on the surface,
house with a boy's face, turned up.

I

Ard na Mara

Catherine and John said it meant beside the sea.
    I thought it meant above,

because the house was above a pasture swooping down
    to the tide, a thirty-foot drop.

You'd step through layers of grass and manure-smell
    to the red, leathery weed splashed

across the rocks, and then looking up, you'd feel dwarfed
    by the one wall left standing —

a fragment of Sweeney's castle — just a stone wing-blade,
    but you got the idea: fortress,

and the fear of raids. Later when I first read the opening
    of the *Agamemnon,* I thought

the Greek signal fires must have been lit on points like this,
    the war won but not over,

the flames a signal to begin learning the next thing to dread.
    The Dobbyns long ago had turned

the hayloft into a room to let. There was a shred of linoleum,
    a cot with spring, and a low sink,

the kind to bathe a baby in. Knives, forks, butane,
    and windows on three walls.

A red door with a latch opened onto cement stairs leading
    down to a toilet in the barn.

Me pissing with the cows, those enormous, contented breathers.
     I spread a sleeping bag

on the cot and slept at an angle so I could look out to the point.
     I had a Hermes Rocket to type on.

The war in Viet Nam still ongoing, but I was well out of it,
     as far as I could get. I went in

to Donegal once a week for newspapers and wine gums.
     For rent I helped John milk the cows

and tend to the hay all through the summer. In return
     I got the earliest hours of the day,

and during storms, the whole afternoon free. I stayed put,
     tried not to leave the farm.

I never saw the ruins of a chapel in the next pasture over,
     and only now have I learned

that a sixth-century monk named Aedh had made his cell
     in the crawlspace there.

Now there are metal roadside markers, and a guidebook
     to his gravestone, an upright bolt

of granite, as tall as I am, rough-hewn, rounded, mossy,
     and chiseled smooth in front.

At the top, like a halo, an incised, long-armed Maltese cross
     in a wide circling rim, a sign,

the book says, of an art in transition, *the pagan monolith
     crowned with Christian radiance.*

To the right and below the wheel is a three-sided Celtic knot—
    symbol of the Trinity—a weave

that makes me imagine Aedh's bones, the arms and legs
    folded neatly over one another.

I stand above him in the mid-day quiet and remember
    how deeply I resented the cars

that sometimes sped by on their way west. I stirred as little
    as I could, sought out no one.

I loved the sweet silence of hay as it cured, and the labor too,
    the mowing and tossing,

letting grass breathe itself dry. Even the raucous, oily baler,
    an old engine with flying ropes,

and compacting magic, dropping bales behind for me
    to pick up and bring in

on the back of a tractor cart. I would heave them to the loft,
    then climb bale upon bale

to wedge them into dusty corners, the weight of each
    locking the other down.

I worked with single-minded intent, the way a calf
    might plunge its nose into a milk pail.

I felt a little like the cows too, the way they knew exactly
    where they belonged. They walked

themselves in from the field, did nothing but chew and stare
    while I fiddled with the milking tubes.

Each summer night was a long prelude and a short darkness.
    I would eat late and alone in my room—

scrambled eggs, rice. I could hear the pub in the village
    warming up as I went to bed between

nine and ten. Sunlight would angle low into the room sometimes,
    and I would feel vaguely visited,

though I could hardly say by what. My knuckles would ache,
    and my breath would quicken,

as if I were late, or had to get somewhere in a hurry,
    though I didn't know where.

I would lie in bed, eyes open, fingers behind my head.
    Though I had nothing to worry about,

I worried. I would watch that light as it passed through
    the window as if it had a mind of its own.

It would reach across my room out to the field and trees
    that stood between me and Aedh

and his grave. In the morning I woke before the cows.
    Sometimes I could see the bay,

but mostly it was a mist or a fog or a shifting cloud cover.
    I would heat water for tea,

and sit at my table and lamp while the sunlight, wherever
    it was, nibbled at the dark.

I wrote in a lined spiral notebook as much as I could.
   I wanted to tell why I joined

and how I came to quit the war. The feeling the words
   gave me was as the light did the night before.

A Place at the Table

It means you can face your accusers.
It means there is no place to hide.
It means you will not drift off to sleep,
or carve your name on your arm.
Or give anyone here the finger.
It means you do not have to wave your hand as if you were drowning.
It means there is nothing here that will drown you.
It means you really do not have to have the answer.
Since there are only a few of you left, sitting across from you,
it means you can study their faces as you would the clouds outside.
You will not totally forget them.
It means you are now, roughly, for a while, just about equal.
In the center before you there is nothing unless someone gives it.
It means that when you are gone, everyone feels it.
It means that when you leave, you feel as if you haven't.
That you still have a place at the table.
Later in your life this moment will return to you as a mote
of dust that floats in on the spars of sunlight.
It will search every room until it finds you.

Half Not

Smell of book-glue, old cardboard,
    and red ink at the edges.
A must almost alive, and a papery feel
    in the air. The summer swirled
in purpled endpapers, cool shelves,
    oiled oak floors. A broad
varnished table of shifty characters,
    and boy detectives with just
enough fear for me to get lost in before
    the required turn back
to the real, where my mother stood
    in line, a return slip stamped
with a gentle thud and inked due-date,
    all the books I wanted
to bring home to our brown bread supper,
    to ears of sweet corn,
and my father on *his* way home.
    He would have stopped
for a taste and thus be late to the table,
    the two of us a little loaded,
the two of us just a bit unsteady,
    me with a book open in my lap,
half under the table, and half not.

Class on Book XI

When we spoke about the return
from the war and how he probed
the beach with his sword, pouring
into the hole a mix of blood, honey,
and wine, we felt a small aperture
opening within the words. Shades
rose to the threshold, some eager
as children let out from school.
Others lingered in the grayness,
their lives burdened with more
than was deserved. We saw some
worth fearing: thick, brutal men
who clutched at what they thought
they were due. Others with furtive
glances wanted to name who was
at fault, who had made amends.
We heard, as if in a room nearby,
a song as gentle to the ear as pages
we turned together. A light wind
carried the notes, but not the words,
and when the song ended, a nylon
jacket sifted from a chair to the floor,
billowing like a sail. It landed softly,
like a friend's touch on the forearm,
turning you in the direction of home.

Credo

"Unholy" in the beginning,

Manhandling the Deity,

through gate and garden,

and bog cotton,

as if it had stopped breathing.

the heart floats like a planet

The eyes are open,

Reason is pared down

for the less than an instant

to thread

I believe

in words alone

and "symphony" to end

your roughed-up book-path

through fields of gorse,

and a world stilled for a second

An instant in which

on nothing.

eager for a flensing.

to a pulse and held off

the words need

one soul to the next.

in such strange incomplete rhymes,

and what lives in between them.

Sum Total

September, my fingers cold.
Folding garage doors wide open.
A digging fork, one tine bent back
by some buried, immovable stone.
In the wooden beams above me,
ants, whole empires and colonies,
chewing wood down to a sawdust
rain. The spiders are fat and happy,
spinning out threads to span the air,
filaments like those we also walk on.
I work at my father's narrow desk,
a stained, pine affair his bills bled
him over. I see him adding things up,
the furrowed sum *not right, not right.*

Night Heron Maybe

I woke to more rain, and felt in the dark
for how wet the sill was, then rolled back
to my radio, and a midnight preacher
in my earphone teaching about sin.

I learned that punishment would come
like lightning that surprises an innocent shore.
Thunder would follow me all my days,
stern reminder and sharp rebuke.

The long, sleek, and pointed call
that rose, as if in response, out of the estuary
of night and storm, said it knew well
what the given world gave, and wanted more.

Camp and Locust

House on the corner where I grew up,
second floor flat I still find in dreams,

window from which I see Candy
squirm out of his collar again.

It is always a lurid, purple night,
the middle of summer. He is taking off,

having figured it out, and is headed toward
all that existence promises, even to dogs.

Philosopher's Stone

From my attic window, school kids coming home,
moving as if to the song I listen to, an antic blues
growl by Van that reminds me of an evening star
one summer under which I am a child digging in dirt
with a spoon, absorbed by a stone I have found.

Unaware of quartz, and of glaciers, and the rocks
that move on their own underground, I believe
I have unearthed something truer than any tale
I have been told. It tells my hand it must not lie
about what it touches, and my tongue the same too.

In Tandem

If winter storms toppled the spruce
that towered over the nursing home
named *Tandem,* you would never dream
of asking me the tree's age, and by that
mean a long life had been good enough.

Nor would you have said at least the tree
did not suffer, and by that mean you would
not think of your own suffering. Instead,
we would have marveled at the pale corona
of roots, the arms uplifted as if in worship.

We would have breathed in the earth smell
and the inner life of the tree, the miracle of
woodcore. We would have been as happy
and curious as squirrels, we who had by then
sworn off the small talk of hope and recovery.

Nobody Too

I would be small and innocuous:
as harmless as the wind
that lifts the grass lightly,
and bends the lupines —
the new stems barely green.

I would pause in affirmation,
like the squirrels in the pine —
my back arching, and torso
rippling into a question
that flees before the answer.

I would teach my heart how to be a heart —
help the doors open wide,
invite the tall shadows to peek in
like curious strangers,
the chambers brimming over — with them.

The Custody of the Eyes

1

On a Sculpture by Lyn Doiron

The eyes are green jewels cut from bottle glass.
The skin blushes with rouge,
as much as plastic allows.
Her hair is hell, blonde hell about to flame.
Had you the desire,
you could rip it from its visible sockets.
She wears a demurely laced collar
and a demi-choker made of pearls.
At center-chest a catacomb to enshrine her heart—
inside of which a kapok hand, palm turned out.
Beneath her waist a swirl of plaster molding
standing in for pubic hair,
but all outside her dress,
and thereby domestic as an apron.
An antique photograph of five women sits upon her belly.
It is a bronze female family gazing
through a temporal aperture,
ready to become, as the mother surely knew:
someday, nothing more than this.
A plain white dress splays against the wall
as backing and frame. Chandelier
spikes to hem, a hint of promenade and ball.
There are no legs for dancing, and nothing else beneath,
as there never was a person here,
just parts topped with cupid lips,
and a stunned green stare.

2

The Origins of the Practice

In some orders the eyes are trained to look neither left nor right
as one walks, but to focus instead on two or three steps ahead.
Cloister manuals might ask one to avoid looking up as a person

enters the room so as to keep the still-point focus of attention.
One could, I suppose, keep any of the senses in custody,
but eyes are naturally unruly, straying without conscience.

Recall the infant's peek-a-boo, the thrill of presence and absence,
or the would-be lover's stolen glance, or the aggression in sizing
someone up, the contempt one senses in an unrelenting stare.

And then there is Agnes, about whom little is certain except
the importance of eyes in her story. Twelve-year-old daughter
of Roman aristocrats, who may themselves have been converts,

she becomes a Christian during the reign of Diocletian
and his persecutions. A prefect's son, who is smitten by her,
and possibly her wealth, proposes marriage, but she refuses,

saying she has already *consecrated her virginity to a spouse,*
who cannot be beheld by mortal eyes. Her conversion is
brought to the attention of a judge who invites her to return

to the pagan and burn incense at the shrine of Minerva.
When she refuses, he threatens her with torture. Fires are lit,
hooks and spikes assembled, but these do not frighten her.

The judge orders her stripped before a crowd in the square,
thinking humiliation will work. But a miracle of visual custody
occurs—the crowd, especially the young men, avert their eyes,

all but one lad, curious and impudent, with lust taking hold.
Instantly he is struck by lightning and blinded. The blow
leaves him convulsing in the square. The lesson, however,

does not end with him. The judge will have to order Agnes
executed. Here the accounts vary widely: she is burned alive,
or beheaded, or given *the gentle death*—a slit artery in the neck.

Perhaps it takes time for the authorities to decide on a method.
As their betters discuss what to do, the ordinary soldiers
pause to look things over. They speak of the child's long hair

that during the day had lengthened into a veil to cover her body.
They marvel at the shackles that keep falling from her tiny wrists.
They puzzle over the fires that won't stay lit. And like soldiers

everywhere, they stand and stare at what they would have to do,
but did not want to do, and would do anyway. This reverie lasts
long enough to make the child herself grow impatient with them.

Agnes calls out toward one who has his sword already drawn:
This lover, she shouts, *this one at last, I confess it, pleases me.
I shall welcome the whole length of his blade into my bosom.*

What are you waiting for, executioner? What are you waiting for?

3

The Day Room

—The elevator to my sister's end of the ward is still broken.

—The back stairs make me feel as if I am doing something forbidden,
though I am not.

—As I climb the three floors I fear a patient is going to jump me—
the wards have men mixed in.

—It must be a childhood fear: what the crazy people will do to you
if they catch you.

—Even now my legs feel heavy with it.

—We are bringing Pat a Christmas sweater. We also have a small tin
crucifix that came for free in the mail.

—When we give it to her, she looks at it as if we had saved her soul—
A kind of joy I am not sure I have ever felt.

—Still it almost redeems this afternoon that has so little natural light.

—When I wheel her down to the day room, the nurse says Pat speaks
of me all the time.

—All the nurses say how we look so much alike, and I say it is our
mother.

—Pat says our mother was in to see her last night.

—I am glad to hear this. No need to say to anyone the decades
our mother has been dead.

—Green jimmies on the cupcakes out on the tray, balloons floating,
    bumping ever so lightly at the ceiling.

—At twenty minutes we are out of things to talk about. TV is on
    a channel of endless caroling.

—Pat loves to sing, sings at the drop of a hat. She knows all the words.
    Easier for her to sing than to speak.

—All the other patients are in the day room by now, most wheeled in
    from the corridor.

—Some are tethered to their chairs, leaning, their eyes rigid and wide.
    I am at a loss for a name for that look.

—I touch my sister's soft gray hair, and I kiss her on the brow.
    Lunch time now, but I say we'll be back soon.

—My eyes are lowered, and I feel nothing but shame at the lie in *soon*.
    I imagine everyone sees right through me.

II

Falsetto

Today we shall look into the mouth of a small cave
     under a city porch, in our vicious mid-winter.

The wind does not quite reach far enough in to touch the cat,
     who is too feral, hungry, and ill to budge.

He is curled up, staring, and waiting things out, ears cocked
     tuned to pipe-thumps, the laundry-warmth.

Elsewhere a judge in our nation has ordered brain medicine
     for a killer, to make him sane enough

to poison or fry tomorrow. The species in charge brims
     with marvels designed to preserve us.

It is war they say, and when they reach in, their lips pucker
     into kissy-sounds, as if they want to fuck you.

Oh, listen to the men of state snapping their fingers, and singing
     slow and sweet enough for us to join.

Hear kitty, kitty, kitty.
     C'mere. C'mere. C'mere.

The Drum Room

The door you come through slams shut before the door you go to opens.

A last stopping place, a once-over from the guard behind his tinted
glass.

Your pockets are empty, wristwatch in the locker, with wallet and
change.

Two pens, a notebook, a wish to act normal, and show you threaten
no one.

It is completely true that you threaten no one.

Nonetheless you feel either you are *in* danger, or that you *are* the danger.

It is a retort designed not to contain, but open and shut like a valve.

A space between entrance and egress, pressure and release.

A moment of pure supplication, a revelation of true marrow and
meaning:

hiatus: opening, rupture, fissure, gap.

A room close to nothing, the reinforced shell of its nothing.

Who here cannot help but think of a plump fly bumping against a
window?

A fly who believes something will give. Something does.

A buzzer, then juice through the wire, and the latches slide in, slide out.

Kritios Boy

1

Hot sheep stink, delicious one another.
The nuzzle of yellowed, matted, oily wool.
Stamp and huddle on the green hillside.
Crowns of clover and clusters of timothy.
The good war just the other side of the valley.
How I love my incipient little life,
and my family flock, most of it.

2

My father and I step through a doorway smell of grease, oil, and gas.
The register is open, the drawer sticking out like a tongue.
A break-in, and who knows what else they got
     or if they are still in there.
My father holds onto my hand tightly, as if it were the cash.

3

The Latin words climb the altar in grape robes
and tied white underthings. The incense
makes my eyes hurt, my cheek sting,
as the priest does, when he slaps me
for forgetting them, the Latin words
that now I remember, have them saved
like nubs of lint in the corner of my pocket.

4

Playing doctor under the porch,
an imaginary world war,

her tending wounded me,
our clothes are coming off.

Summer morning, and heavy wash hung out.

No one knows where we are.
A row of light slants in,
a narrow stripe that falls
across every secret we have.

Wherever the light falls,
that will be where we touch.
We won't tell anyone. We promise.

    5

I am wide-awake, flat on my back,
waiting for the vast river of an eclipse
    to wash over the moon.
The whorl of planets, a gristly wheel of trees.
Reason is back in the house still clutching its slate,
    ever the schoolboy eager.

    6

Red orb of the sacred heart,
    thorn-entwined,
a fist bleeding down the plaster robe.

The gold tabernacle open,
    bereft.
A smoking, peppery censer,

the devout around me abject,
     almost grieving.
A steady *sssh* of nylons as they approach.

Flecks of lipstick on the teeth,
     wet tongues
tense, and uplifted.

7

I am fifteen and trusted.
I slide a pail on wheels across the office floor,
across linoleum worn to the wood.
I bring a swirl of mop, a cloud of ammonia.
A clean water rinse and a sprinkle of Joy,
like no joy I know of.
The pastel smell hovers over
all the files and stays on my fingers.
Puckered up, ridged, lemon-sweet.

8

A war is on.
You want to go and see it,
but you have to wait before you begin,
so you get day jobs out of the union hall.
You lift forelegs and hinds of beef at the siding dock.
First you hook one end, and wrap your arms around the other.
Then put your belly underneath, to keep the meat from sliding out.
The butcher's smock gets caked and stiff with grease.
You think dead meat is the real thing, smelling of the real.
It is foul enough to make you think it is everlasting.

9

Thus my own free-standing self-creation:
legs contra-posto, to denote ease in the world,
the pelvis angled diagonally upward, to connote Eros,
ribs all moving with my breath, to mean heart,
lips no longer frozen in a smile. I am not a man yet,
but ready for any job or love or war you've got.

Brasso

Sweet, waxy smell,
and the opaque film it
dries to. Here is a tissue
wrapped around the thumb,
and here the coal-black
residue it lifts, as if from
the watery depth of a tarn.
It is an *is what it should be,*
as neutral as a crease,
as certain as a salute,
as true as the alignment
of buckle with shirt buttons
and fly. And here are boots
under a slow, circular finger
and spit. Here too a mindless
attention-standing for hours
at the rack, skivvies billowing
out whitely. People will die
because of you, your mistakes,
so says the sergeant under arms,
so says my face memorizing
orders in tiny mirrors of brass,
so says my feet at forty-five
degrees, so says my chin
tucked in, and my thumbs
at the seams, if flesh ever had
a seam, so says my torso to
the green foot-locker with
my effects designated personal,
and so says, so says, so says
that box back to me as I note
that without a tray it is large
enough for a child to be buried in.

Conscientious Objector Discharge

You will have to take a last physical, fill out a set of insurance forms.

You will need a lawyer to clear you, and a shrink to say you are sane,
   but they both know that already and are secretly glad to do
      something against this war.

Maybe a friend at the bursar's to make sure you get your back pay.

Someone in personnel will open up three afternoons of sunlight leave,
   and two nights in between.

You should savor it at Denny's where the stupid, endless menu seems
   as bright as your future might be with the waitress.

Then in the morning of your last minute in, maybe around ten a.m.,
   the one hour when no one needs to get hurt anywhere,

you will stand in a line before a corporal's desk. You will tell them
   for the last time that yes you are certain

and no you will not do this anymore. The floorboards will groan,
   but they will not be grieving.

Go ahead, take what you are given this day, fold it into a creased half,
   and put that paper in your wallet.

Knock on the doorframe and step out. Your feet as they hit the gravel
   will make it chatter.

You should listen to it—listen hard to this path you are on.
   It will sound as if you are walking on water.

For the Matinee

Stand here in the line for the aged and infirm,
    and praise the living light of the movie.

Enter at the rising of the credits, the roll call
    of who did what and for whom.

Praise this noon when we get lost to the world.
    No one needs to know where we are.

Strike it from the record. Let there be no more talk
    of what we should have done.

Or done better. Forget the limits of the lives we have lived.
    Forget those lives.

Fold and pile the flaws on the seats between us.
    There is room.
    Let us nod to each other.

Democratic Vista

in memoriam Saul Bellow

Third Day

since you died.
You would attach nothing to the number.
You would lean your head back laughing if anyone did.

So I will count it up this way:
this be the day after the day after the day.

Neither earth nor sky has begun to notice,
as you would have predicted.

You once said that if words would pay
close enough attention to the body,
then the soul would follow.

Here lyeth the body.

Words for Faraj

A woman is lost in delirium at the platform edge,
saying that no one would understand, and she is right.

On the train a father whispers with his eyes to his son
across the aisle, the son looking away.

There must be more words for God than snow.
A flag will flicker in the slightest wind.

I listen to you confess to confessions coerced,
you saying torture can be a doorway, and the pain

in a mock hanging lasts only until the lights go out.
When they wake you what hurts the most is

that the afterlife should seem so ugly and familiar.
Under your chin faint traces of a line, as if the scar

wants to disappear, be camouflaged by folds of neck
and the cartilage we name for Adam and the apple.

Palm Reading

Mine the delicate hands of my mother.
The little finger reminds me of bones
in a chicken-wing. My knuckles ache,
a nerve is damaged, and my daily labors
are soft, sedentary, and devoid of callus.

When I was a student I shook the hand
of a poet I admired. It was so soft, I felt
significantly superior to him, I who knew
the world of hard men and heavy-lifting.
Now my hands are joined with his.

Even my penmanship has no firmness,
as if I lacked a clarity of purpose.
Keats sometimes separated each letter
in a word, as if he wanted the silences
within the word to become audible.

The haunting hand in his poem floats
me toward his final Roman room.
I imagine him staring at the grain
of the wooden bed, its swirl of lines,
the feeling that here was perfect form.

Think Frederick, *fried-reich*,
free and peaceful ruler,
son of the sullen working class.
Think of his plaster mask you could not touch.
Think how little time your delicate hands have left.

Balpeen Hammer

He lay sideways on the bed,
the flimsy curtains on their runners
stirring when the nurses rushed by.

They did not plan to admit him,
meaning he would die here soon.
I leaned on the bedrail and watched

his breath enter and leave.
It seemed easy, but he was in a coma,
so who could say?

I dabbed at his parched lips
with a swab until a nurse gave me
a grape popsicle. "Keep an eye on it."

No telling how long it would be.
No telling if he knew I was doing this,
but I am sure how good it tasted.

I rested the ice on his tongue,
but held the weight off,
balanced it in my hand.

I remembered a balpeen hammer,
a miniature, the size of a popsicle,
my favorite among all his tools.

There was no claw at the back,
but round steel, for *peening,*
the shaping and smoothing of metal.

That's how I wanted his minutes
to pass, no thrash or heave,
just a steady tapping away until done.

The Salt Stronger

I have seen the legislators
on their way,
the jacketless men
in mid-winter who will cast
their votes like stones for this war.

Men who have to cross the street
through slush
and over gutter, their cuffs
now vaguely blued with a salt
that dries in dots where it splashes,

and mingles with the finely
woven cloth
of the chalk-stripe suits,
the *soi-disant* practical men,
you can see them now tiptoeing,

now leaping, balletic, windsor-knotted,
fragrant
and shaved,
they pass, they pass
the window of the Capitol Deli

wherein I am writing to my friend
in Baghdad,
he a "witness for peace,"
a poet who for years has wondered
what good poetry is or has been or does.

I compose today's answer from here,
saying,

I think of poetry
as a salt dug from a foreign mine
that arrives like a miracle in Boston

as pellets to break underfoot
and melt
the dangerous plated ice
and cling to the acknowledged lawmakers,
to stay with them in their dreams,

to eat at the cloth and reach down
to the skin
and beyond the calf
into the shin. I think the soul
is equivalent to bone, and that conscience

must hide in the marrow,
float in the rich fluids
and wander the honeycomb at the center.
There, and not in the brain,
or even the heart is where

the words attach, where they land
and settle,
take root after the long
passage through the body's by-ways.
Just think, I write, *of how some poetry rolls*

off the tongue, then try to see the tongue
in the case
that faces me, a curious,
thick extension of cow-flesh
fresh from a butcher's block, grainy and flush.

I think that if my tongue alone could talk
it would swear
in any court that poetry
tastes like the iodine in blood,
or the copper in spit, and makes a salt stronger than tears.

III

Against Epiphany

What god was it that would open
earth's picture book and see the two
of us on a road, snowfields glittering
on every side and poplars bent like
the fingers of an old man clutching
what he loved about the sun?

Which one was it that would peer
into our thatched, white-washed
farmhouse, and see the fur, flies,
and shit-stained walls? Which one
laughed at the barbed wire fences,
the wall topped with broken glass?

Which of the many who came then,
gleaming and rimed in hard sunlight?
Which of those who bobbed like ice
along the winter shore? What did
we have that any god would want?
Quick, if you can find it, hide it.

Agricola, Agricolae

No one could tell what the spell was that came over us
    while the war lingered on.

Not the orange "feeder" fish that multiplied,
    nor the Stellar's jay that made cartwheel landings.

We learned later the poison was also found in the midnight
    blue of our delphinium,

and in the blue optimism of glaciers at their base,
    where they advance when no one is looking.

Traces too were found in the blue veins of a marble
    you sometimes see in the capital.

We were in the grip of a torment we did not understand.
    When we launched our arrows to heaven,

nothing could stop them, not gravity, not flesh, not even
    the parched earth where they landed.

    These were our arrows. This was our world.

Archilochus

1

I don't care what they did.
I don't care what we believe.
I've got nothing left to give.

2

...] no
...] job
...] future
...] barbaric
...] faith

3

At the place where three roads meet.
At night, and in the cold.
Where I walk up and down beside the cars.
Where I shimmy the jingle in the Dunkin's cup.
Where I carry a cardboard sign,
the magic marker marking the magic:
help keep this homeless vet good and drunk.

4

My plastic beach chair,
I set this baby up anywhere.
Right now I am on what they call an island.
It is tended in the summer by the gardeners of the good.
My objective? My point in sitting here?
To be honest, I would, sir, like to plow your daughter.

5

I wouldn't trade this for anything.

not today   not for anyone

6

For the thirteen days before we went to Iraq,
I thought we'd all gone crazy.
All those immaculate white shirts, and pastel ties,
the lapels laden with flags made with jewels,
mostly rubies.

7

Gray [. . .
papery [. . .
oval [. . .
hive [. . .
spring [. . .

8

Now the stinging wasp wings from its cell.
The feeler, and the feet, tickling your cheek.

The Black Dog

Adrenaline howling in my head,
the black dog was my brain...

—Les Murray, "Corniche"

Beware the red taxi bleeding like a fresh wound.
And walkers who know what waits for them.

Beware stern yellow flames, the destiny that blisters all,
and little signs hung from lamp-poles like fascists.

Beware the bulbs formed into the outline of a man crossing the street.
Beware his elbows, his feet, and his soul.

Beware anyone who tells you the signs are right or that he is guiltless.
Beware the black dog at your feet.

He thinks you are in trouble, and wants to help.
He thinks you are going to kick him, or break his neck.

He thinks you are the trouble, so he bares his teeth.
He raises his lips to show you how much he cares.

How much he loves your life and would do anything to save you.
Beware him, because he will devour you.

Beware the wordless sounds he makes.
Beware his ghostly body, especially when it looks like me.

It is said in the annals that if you see him, you must kill him.
Or tell someone else about him.

If you fail to do this, you will die,
and great harm will come to your entire family.

A Diagnosis of Ibis

At this pond nothing gathers anymore—
neither nesting eagle, nor the newt in mottle.

    It is more, and worse, than that.

What was wondrous inside has all but fled.
Her mind, her precise, bountiful mind—

    drained to a stubble of tree, moss, mud.

Here's a white feather of what used to be here,
the strands—long, delicate axons,

    tissue of nerve—tissue of flesh and light.

From the house I watch her gun the engine.
It is Monday morning. She has to be somewhere.

    The engine roars, eases, roars, eases.

Her mind steps through the shallows on stilted legs.
The mud soft, the water flowing out,

    the reeds relenting, bending over, ready.

She comes back in and says I don't know what to do.
The sun, the air, the rest of the elements, and I,

    we all say, me too.

Cicada

That whine is the sound
of waste, rot, the frantic,
grinding inability to attend
to anything but sere thwarting
of yourself, a dry corrosion
which some say they know,
but you and I —

(my jaw clenched as you
turn a page,
you with a heart like drywall,
I who would
lace my arms with razors,
then press them
slowly to your lips,
the metal taste
mixing with flesh,
and through gritted teeth
I making the sound
of you, you, you
do not know, meaning
only me, me)

we know best.

Luna

moonlight did not find us out inside

did not lift our walls from their floors

or shift the house off the foundation

did not melt the wood down to soggy

cardboard then roll us off the rim

of the world did not promise us more

than light shined on her palm, or cuts

on her fingers rimmed with dirt did not

walk us to the end of the pasture or point

out the leaning Neolithic slabs the animal

burrow the entrance smooth did not light

the torch by which we saw on the ceiling

the deer in herds the long-horned cattle

galloping to the secret room where a stick

figure man lay near a bison speared

its insides spilling out and the shapely

bird atop the staff his rude icon of hope

a blessing the moon had no idea was there

Note Held

"Nothing but sunlight and gleaming,
linoleum flecked with flame,
a thick coat of wax that flashed
down a corridor and led to a room,
a place where I curled up a few
innocuous inches off the floor.
Straps — word out of strophe,
the restraints of line and stanza —
straps hung in loops on closet hooks.
On the nightstand a basket with
peanut butter crackers, a vivid
and unnatural orange, a crinkly
wrap. A knee-high fridge stocked
with icy juices, foil boxes, straws
glued on. A female voice next door
claimed she was still a human being,
though I could not hear the reasons.
When it was my turn, I answered
right away, saying I knew where
I was and why. No, I would not
harm myself, surprised to be asked
as I had never had the thought.
Yes I knew where I was going next.
Out the window and through shadow
and streetlight, I saw how this building
connected to the next. I was to follow
a stripe painted on the wall. Someone
would walk with me as well. I felt fine
I said, and it was sort of true. Actually
I felt nailed by one wrist to a desire
to flee and by the other to a sincere

longing for sleep. I was not in pain.
Thank you. I felt like the very last note
in a concert, the one that hovers as if
it wants to linger, but is already over."

The Looking House Stanza

When the melancholia blew in
like a storm off the North Atlantic
the ground we walked on sloped
all the way down to the little we
could remember, grew slippery
with loose pebbles of everything
we wanted to forget. We watched
a wild scattering of loss unfold —
the lives we had wanted to live,
or lived once, all falling away
into mists thick enough to hide
the sheep, and make their bleating
sound like a mind in distress.
We waded in rainwater, rivers
of inexplicable fear, and it was
not from sadness we took refuge
in the lee of a ruin, a slate hut
herders were forced to abandon
in famine. A hillside of reminders
of how little we knew about fatal
sorrow, and indignity without end.
We gathered what we could imagine
of suffering of such focus and density
it seemed sent to re-make the world
into fog, and reduce lives to shivers
so vicious no one could stop shaking.
Hope stared at nothing, with nothing
forthcoming. In a room without roof,
by a window minus its wall, I saw
a mind I loved could no longer go on.
I would have sheltered you from all,

but there was nothing but rain and wind
to hold onto. I blustered, I swore,
I shook you by the shoulders, thinking
there must be something I can do.

Small Land Animals

heads bowed—eyes trained on the given earth—
    what are they thinking?

even in the striking down—the long veins of the neck—
    with you

red-tail fox—the wariness of a wing-foot dream —
    write back soon

glimmering retinas of night—first thought and last—
    tell me tell me

last night home, before I—hours under the chenille—
    feral

sweet-water stream—a bed of gravel and saw grass—
    a gull dogs have gotten into

nerve running down the leg—twitching in the eye—
    and chipmunks at the door

halfway down a hole—dragged you back by the scruff—
    sorry

the one thing needed—a cardinal leapt into the air—
    the pasture saw

pale woolly tatters on the wire—a lamb slipped out—
    or squeezed back in

the split lip infinitive—a blood that pools in every mouth—
    am   *is*   *are*

Pinckney Street

A view from the crest of Boston to the river—
a walk and my friend stopping to say that
for three weeks each year
and beginning tomorrow
this will be the most
beautiful place in the city—
our respite in the brick-faced buildings
blushing in sunlight,
in star magnolias swelling,
about to burst into bright badges,
medallions of tangible life and light
the shook foil that Hopkins wrote about—
the minutes we have of grandeur, hope, gratitude.

First Song Again

Trust all the wood you stand on,
Become an ally of the grain,
    Bend in the wind.

Trust even the high, precarious places,
The steeples and windy overhangs
    That teach you everything.

Trust too the rose-tint of late afternoon
Sifting down through a lofted
    Blue heron wing.

Trust above all the imminent return
Of the small, but persistent
    Impulse to sing.

Notes

"Credo" is for John F. Deane.

"In Tandem" is for Betty Rose Rubin.

"The Custody of the Eyes" is for Mary Pat Brown.

1

Lyn Doiron's sculpture was exhibited at The Harbor Gallery, University of Massachusetts–Boston, in June 2001.

2

There are many and varied accounts of the martyrdom of St. Agnes. The tale told here is adapted primarily from *The Lives of the Saints* by Alban Butler (1709–1773), *Crowns of Martyrdom* by Aurelius Prudentius Clemens (348–c. 413), and *Notes Concerning Virginity*, by St. Ambrose (338–397).

"Words for Faraj" is for Faraj Sarkohi, an Iranian editor and fiction writer who lives now in exile after repeated imprisonments.

"The Salt Stronger" is for Ted Sexauer.

"Archilochus" refers to the early Greek lyric poet by the same name. Born c. 680 BCE on the island of Paros, the historical Archilochus was a mercenary as well as an earthy, non-heroic, often satirical poet.

"Pinckney Street" is for James Carroll.

Acknowledgments

I wish to thank sincerely the editors of the following journals, where earlier versions of some of the poems in this book first appeared: *AGNI, The American Poetry Review, Connecticut Poetry Review, Diner, FIELD, Harvard Review, Image, The Irish Times, Journal of Modern Writing, Literary Imagination, New American Writing, Peacework, Perihelion, Ploughshares, Poetry, Poetry Ireland Review, Poetry Porch, Poet's Market, Post Road, Provincetown Arts, Salamander, Sow's Ear Review,* and *Writer's Digest.*

The following poems, or earlier versions of them, sometimes with different titles, appeared in *House on Water, House in Air: New and Selected Poems* (Dublin, Ireland, Dedalus Press, 2002): "Against Epiphany," "Diagnosis of Ibis," "First Song Again," "House on Water, House in Air," "Kritios Boy" (sections 1 and 4), "Luna," "Night Heron Maybe," "Note Held," "The Custody of the Eyes" (section 1), "The Sum Total," and "Words for Faraj."

An earlier version of "Night Heron Maybe" was collected in *Cabin Fever* (Washington, DC: The Word Works, 2003).

For advice and inspiration as these poems came into being, I want to thank Jenny Barber, Eva Bourke, Kevin Bowen, James Carroll, Martha Collins, John F. Deane, Ken Greenberg, Joan Houlihan, George Kalogeris, Maxine Hong Kingston, Fiona McCrae, David Rivard, Stefi Rubin, Jeff Shotts, and Kaethe Weingarten.

FRED MARCHANT is the author of three other books of poetry: *Tipping Point,* which won the 1993 Washington Prize, *House on Water, House in Air: New and Selected Poems* (Dedalus Press, Dublin, Ireland), and *Full Moon Boat* (Graywolf Press). Co-translator (with Nguyen Ba Chung) of *From a Corner of My Yard* by the Vietnamese poet Tran Dang Khoa, he has also edited and written a critical introduction for *Another World Instead: The Early Poems of William Stafford, 1937–1947.* Marchant is the Director of the Creative Program and The Poetry Center at Suffolk University in Boston, Massachusetts.

This text of *The Looking House* is set in Adobe Caslon Pro, an open type version of a typeface originally designed by William Caslon sometime between 1720 and 1766. The Adobe version was drawn by Carol Twombly in 1989.

Book design by Wendy Holdman.
Composition by BookMobile Design and Publishing Services,
    Minneapolis, Minnesota.
Manufactured by BookMobile on acid-free paper.